Wild Predators!

Wolves and Other Dogs

Andrew Solway

First published in Great Britain by
Heinemann Library, Halley Court, Jordan Hill,
Oxford OX2 8EJ, part of Harcourt Education.
Heinemann is a registered trademark of Harcourt
Education Ltd.

Editorial: Lucy Thunder and Harriet Milles
Design: David Poole and Paul Myerscough
Illustrations: Geoff Ward
Picture Research: Rebecca Sodergren,
Melissa Allison and Pete Morris
Production: Séverine Ribierre

Originated by Ambassador Litho Ltd
Printed and bound in Hong Kong and China by
South China Printing Co. Ltd.
The paper used to print this book comes from
sustainable resources.

ISBN 0 431 18995 1
08 07 06 05 04
10 9 8 7 6 5 4 3 2 1

British Library Cataloguing in Publication Data
Solway, Andrew
Wolves and Other Dogs. – (Wild predators)
 599.7′73153
A full catalogue record for this book is available
from the British Library.

Acknowledgements
The Publishers would like to thank the following
for permission to reproduce photographs:
Ardea/Jean Paul Ferrero p**37**; Ardea/Wardene
Weisser p**30**; BBC Natural History Unit/Peter
Blackwell p**26**; CORBIS/Randy Wells p**13**top;
CORBIS/Alissa Crandall p**20**; CORBIS/Carl and Ann
Purcell p**17** top; CORBIS/D Robert & Lori Franz
p**23** top; CORBIS/Gallo p**15** top; CORBIS/Gallo
Images p**42**; CORBIS/Joe Mcdonald p**6**;
CORBIS/Martin Harvey p**15** bottom; CORBIS/Paul
A.Souders p**31** top; Digital Vision p**7l**; Frank Lane
Picture Agency/Fritz Polking p**27**; Frank Lane
Picture Agency/Gerard Lacz p**10**; Frank Lane
Picture Agency/Jurgen and Christine Sohns p**36**;
Frank Lane Picture Agency/Mark Newman p**11**;
Frank Lane Picture Agency/Minden Pictures pp**9**,
22, **43**; Frank Lane Picture Agency/Robert Canis
p**19** right; Frank Lane Picture Agency/S & D & K
Maslowski pp**28**, **29**; Frank Lane Picture
Agency/Terry Whittaker pp**34**, **39**; NHPA/Peter
Pickford p**16**; NHPA/Dan Griggs p**19** top;
NHPA/Henry Ausloos p**23** bottom; Natural History
Picture Library/J & A Scott pp**40**, **41**; NHPA/John
Shaw p**13** bottom; NHPA/K Ghani p**38**; Natural
History Picture Library/Laurie Campbell p**5** top;
NHPA/Martin Harvey p**14**; NHPA/T Kitchen &
V Hurst p**7**; Natural Visions/Jason Venus p**21**
right; NHPA/Haroldo Palo Jr p**32**; NHPA/Daryl
Balfour p**17** bottom; Oxford Scientific Films/Nick
Gordon p**35**; Oxford Scientific Films/Rick Price/SAL
p**31** bottom; SPL/Anthony Mercieca p**24**; SPL/Art
Wolfe p**33**; SPL/Nigel Dennis p**25**; SPL/Pat & Tom
Leeson p**21** top; SPL/Jeff Lepore p**4**; SPL/Sandford
& Agliolo p**18**; SPL/Tim Davis p**5** bottom;
SPL/William Ervin pp**8**, **12**

Cover photograph of a North American
grey wolf reproduced with permission of
NHPA (John Shaw). Title page photograph of a
white wolf snarling reproduced with permission of
CORBIS.

The Publishers would like to thank Michael Bright,
Senior Producer, BBC Natural History Unit, for his
assistance in the preparation of this book.

Every effort has been made to contact copyright
holders of any material reproduced in this book.
Any omissions will be rectified in subsequent
printings if notice is given to the Publishers.

Contents

Any words appearing in the text in bold, **like this**, are explained in the Glossary.

Adaptable predators

We have very different feelings about domestic (pet) dogs and their wild relations. Dogs live in our homes, and some, such as sheep and cattle dogs, do important jobs for us. But the howling of a wolf sends a shiver down the spine, and most farmers will shoot a fox or a coyote on sight. Dogs, wolves, foxes and coyotes are all part of the same **family** – the dogs or **canids** (family Canidae). Wild or tame, all of them are **predators** to be reckoned with.

What makes a canid?

Wolves and other canids belong to a larger group of **mammals** called **carnivores** (order Carnivora). All carnivores have scissor-like back teeth for slicing through flesh. Most canids are built for long-distance running. They have long legs and a deep chest, which gives them stamina (staying power). Canids cannot retract their claws, as cats can. Because they are always scraping on the ground, a canid's claws are blunt. They are used for grip and to hold down **prey**, rather than as weapons.

Hearing, eyesight and smell are important senses for canids. Their eyes work well both during the day and at night. African wild dogs, which live on open plains, rely particularly on their eyes for finding prey. Other canids rely more on smell or hearing. **Nocturnal** hunters, such as foxes, have particularly good hearing, and listen for their prey.

Canids, like this wolf, have large, pointed teeth called canines at the front of the mouth for stabbing into their prey. At the back of the mouth are scissor-like, meat-cutting teeth.

Scavengers

Although they are predators, most canids are very adaptable about what they eat. Foxes, for instance, will live entirely on mice, voles or rabbits if there is a good supply. But they will also **scavenge** and eat fruit, insects, worms or almost any other food. This adaptability helps different kinds of canid to survive in a wide range of **habitats**, from the Arctic to the Sahara Desert.

Foxes are especially good at adapting to what food is available. In autumn they eat fruit, and they will eat insects and even hunt worms, as this fox is doing.

Domestic dogs and wolves

Pet dogs are direct **descendants** of wolves that were **domesticated** by humans about 15,000 years ago. The earliest known fossil of a domestic dog is about 14,000 years old. These early dogs probably looked like dingoes (see page 36). Today there are many different kinds of domestic dogs. People have **bred** different kinds of dog for different purposes. Long-legged wolfhounds and greyhounds, for instance, were bred as fast-running hunters, while short-legged terriers were bred to go down animal burrows. Beagles, like this one, were bred to hunt by smell. Although there are huge differences between different kinds of dog, all of them belong to the same **species** – Canis familaris.

Grey wolf

When the pack first attacks, the moose charges at its attackers. But the wolves leap away before it can get near. The moose wheels around and charges again, then it panics and begins to run. The wolves follow, leaping at its back and sides. Soon the repeated attacks take their toll, and the moose slows down. The pack leader chooses his moment, then goes for the moose's throat.

Biggest in the family

Grey wolves are the biggest animals in the **canid family**. A large wolf can be 1.5 metres long not counting its tail, 1 metre high at the shoulder and can weigh 75 kilograms. Male wolves are bigger than females.

Small populations of grey wolves live in Europe, the Middle East and the USA, but most live in northern North America, and in Russia and central Asia.

Packing together

Wolves usually live and hunt in packs (groups). These are usually made up of around 6 or 7 wolves, but can be more. At the core of the pack are an adult male and female that have **mated** and produced young. This pair – the alpha pair – are the pack leaders. Other wolves in the pack may be family members – offspring of the alpha pair that have grown up. But other wolves from outside the family group may also be accepted into the pack.

Wolves are best known for hunting **prey** in packs, but they also hunt alone for smaller prey such as lemmings, hares, beavers and voles.

A new family

The alpha male and female mate in the winter months. The rest of the pack helps to feed and protect the alpha pair's cubs, to give them the best chance of survival. In early spring the alpha pair find or dig a den – a hole or cave. About 9 weeks after mating the female gives birth. Usually she will produce 5 or 6 cubs.

At first, a wolf cub's eyes are closed, it cannot hear and it is very weak. At first the cubs feed on their mother's milk every 2 hours, and the female remains with them in the den. After about a fortnight the cubs' eyes open, and the female spends less time with them.

Grey wolves are not always grey – their coat can vary from white to jet-black. Most Arctic wolves, for instance, are white or yellowish.

Wolves around the world

Although grey wolves are all one **species** there are several types in different parts of the world. Arctic wolves are found in the far north: they are the biggest wolves. Common wolves are medium-sized and live in the forests of Europe and Asia, while timber wolves are medium-sized wolves found in North America. Steppe wolves are small wolves that live in grassland (steppe) in Russia.

A wolf mother with her cubs. The cubs' eyes are blue at first, but they gradually change to the yellow of an adult.

Defending the territory

While the alpha female is with her cubs in the den, the rest of the pack establish a **territory** around it. This is an area in which the pack can find enough food and water to feed themselves and the new cubs. The pack defends this territory against other wolves. They mark the borders by **scent-marking** – leaving droppings or patches of **urine** on prominent spots such as trees or large rocks. Other wolves can tell from these scent marks that a pack has claimed the area.

By about 2 months old the cubs are playing outside the den. At this point they are ready to eat meat. The other pack members begin to help feeding the cubs. They catch food and eat it, then come back to the den and **regurgitate** some for the cubs.

Autumn and winter

By autumn the cubs are well grown and can travel with the pack, although they are not yet big enough to help in the hunting. At this time of year some of the young wolves that were born the previous year may leave, hoping to find a **mate** and begin their own pack.

In northern areas, important prey animals such as caribou travel to their breeding grounds in autumn. Wolf packs in these areas move to follow their prey.

When wolves make a large kill, the alpha wolves get to eat first, followed by wolves in the next rank, and so on.

Musk oxen protect their calves from a wolf pack by forming a defensive ring of adults, with the calves in the middle. The wolves try to break the ring in one place, then dash in and grab a calf.

Hunting in a pack

Wolves live together in packs because by working together they can catch large prey such as moose, elk, deer, goats, bison and musk oxen. When they hunt alone they usually catch smaller **mammals** such as lemmings or hares. In winter many small animals **hibernate**, so wolves can eat better by hunting in a pack. A caribou or moose may take more effort to catch than a lemming, but it will feed the whole pack for several days.

Wolves are clever animals, and they need all their intelligence for successful hunting. They first find their prey through smell, either by following a scent trail on the ground or picking up the scent of prey in the air. The wolves move towards this scent, trying to get as close as possible without the prey noticing. Deer and moose can outrun a wolf if they have a reasonable start, but if the wolves can get close before they attack the prey is unlikely to escape.

If the wolves are attacking a herd of animals such as deer, they will look for a straggler outside the main herd. With all large prey they begin by attacking the flanks (sides) and rump (rear) to weaken the animal. Then one wolf, usually the alpha male, will go for the animal's nose or throat.

Keeping in touch

Wolves need to communicate when hunting, and also to avoid conflict within the pack. A wolf's expression and body language say a lot to other wolves. When one wolf is **dominant** over another, the dominant wolf stands with ears erect and tail high, whereas the lower ranking wolf half-crouches with ears back, tail between legs and lips pulled back in a 'smile'. When a cub begins a rough and tumble, it puts on a 'play expression', to show that it is not serious about the fighting.

Touch and smell are also important in wolf communication. Scent marks are used to mark out territory, and wolves in the same pack greet each other by rubbing their heads together, or by smelling or licking each other. These daily contacts help to strengthen the bonds between pack members.

Wolves keep in touch at a distance by howling. This is particularly important in forests, where it is hard to see far. Wolves also sometimes howl together to show their strength to neighbouring packs.

Howling is one way that wolves can communicate over long distances. Each wolf has its own distinctive howl.

Saving wolves

At one time, grey wolves were spread throughout North America, Europe and Asia. But in some areas humans have wiped out wolves, and in other areas there are only small populations left. People hunt wolves for sport, farmers kill wolves because they fear they will eat their **livestock**, and much of the land that wolves once lived on has been cleared for farming or to build towns and cities.

In parts of North America and Europe the wolf is now protected, and in a few of these protected areas their numbers are gradually increasing. In places such as Yellowstone Park in the USA, wolves were wiped out completely in the past, but conservation workers have now reintroduced them by bringing in wolves from elsewhere. However, there is still a long way to go before wolves and people can live together in harmony.

In this picture the top wolf is dominant, as shown by its erect ears and high tail. The other wolf is showing submission by lying down, ears back, and tucking its tail between its legs.

Red wolves

In the eastern USA, there was in the past a **species** of wolf with a reddish colour to its coat, known as the red wolf. Today these red wolves have almost completely died out, with only a few remaining in captivity. However, new studies suggest that some of the 'grey wolves' in south-eastern Canada may in fact be red wolves, or **hybrids** of red and grey wolves. And some 'coyotes' may be hybrids of red wolves and coyotes. There are also programmes to reintroduce this **endangered** species into its old habitat.

Coyote

The coyote has been following the badger all night. Now the badger has found a rabbit burrow and is digging open the entrance. Soon a rabbit pops out of another hole and begins to run. The coyote gives chase, and within a few minutes it is eating supper.

Growing population

Coyotes are smaller and slimmer than wolves. They are 45 to 63 centimetres tall at the shoulder, with a narrow muzzle and long, slender legs. Originally coyotes were grassland animals, living in western America. But as wolf populations in America dropped, coyotes grew in numbers and moved into new areas. They can now be found in much of North and Central America.

Wily hunters

Coyotes usually hunt at night and they rely on their keen sense of smell to follow **prey**. They mainly eat **rodents** and rabbits, but they also eat birds, lizards, fruit, and larger prey such as deer. Coyotes also kill farm **livestock**, especially sheep. For this reason farmers regularly kill them.

Even in the snow, a coyote's super-sensitive nose can follow the scent of a small animal to its burrow.

Coyotes hunt in different ways. When hunting mice or rats, coyotes stalk their prey until they are close enough to pounce. When hunting fast-moving prey such as a jackrabbit, they chase their victim until it is exhausted. To catch large prey, coyotes usually hunt in packs.

Living in packs

Coyotes **mate** in the winter, and this is also the time when they most often hunt large prey, so in winter they often live together in packs. As with wolves, an alpha male and female lead the pack, and these are the only pair to **breed**.

Coyotes are the noisiest of all the **canids**. They howl to advertise their presence to other coyotes, yelp when playing, and bark as a threat when protecting a den.

A coyote pack defends a **territory** and marks its boundaries with **scent marks**. The size of territory a pack needs varies according to how rich the area is in food. It may be over 100 square kilometres (40 square miles), or as small as 3 square kilometres (1 square mile).

Bringing up pups

Female coyotes give birth about 9 weeks after mating. Coyote pups are born helpless, but become active soon after their eyes open at 2 weeks old. From about 3 weeks the male helps to feed the pups. Other pack members guard the pups, but do not help with feeding.

From about 8 or 10 weeks old, the young coyotes go on hunting trips. In autumn some young coyotes leave the pack, but some may stay on for another year.

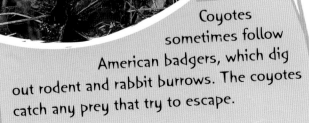

Coyotes sometimes follow American badgers, which dig out rodent and rabbit burrows. The coyotes catch any prey that try to escape.

Ethiopian wolf

As the female wolf trots up to the low cliff, three cubs come bounding out of a small cave. The cubs leap at their mother, whining and licking her muzzle. After a few moments the mother **regurgitates** some food, and the cubs fall on it eagerly.

Highland wolves

Ethiopian wolves (also known as Simien jackals or Abyssinian wolves) are found only on high moorlands in a few mountainous areas of Ethiopia. They are long-legged but lightly built, with large ears, a narrow muzzle and small teeth. Their coat is reddish, with white underparts, and they have a white tip to their tail.

The main **prey** of Ethiopian wolves are giant mole rats and grass rats. Most of the time the wolves hunt alone and when they spot a victim, they sneak up quietly before making a final short dash to grab the prey. Although Ethiopian wolves hunt alone, they live in packs. They do this to protect their **rodent**-rich **territory**. Every morning and evening the wolves patrol the borders of their territory, leaving **scent marks** as a sign of ownership. Sometimes there are disputes between neighbouring packs during these patrols. These involve lots of growling and barking, but there is rarely a fight.

Ethiopian wolves look more like tall foxes than wolves. However, modern studies suggest that they are closely related to grey wolves and coyotes.

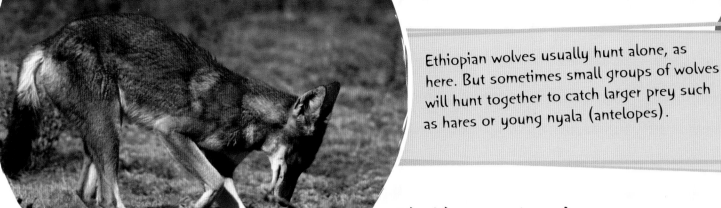

Ethiopian wolves usually hunt alone, as here. But sometimes small groups of wolves will hunt together to catch larger prey such as hares or young nyala (antelopes).

Mating and cubs

Unlike grey wolf packs, Ethiopian wolf packs do not have a **mating** pair at their centre. The reason for this is that all the members of the pack are close relatives, and if they mated it would lead to **inbreeding**. Instead, the **dominant** female in each pack almost always mates with a male from a neighbouring pack.

As with wolves and coyotes, the female gives birth in a den. The pups feed on her milk for the first 4 weeks, after which they begin to eat regurgitated food. Other pack members then help to feed the cubs. The cubs continue to be fed by the pack until they are 6 months old.

Close to extinction

Ethiopian wolves are found in only a few small areas, and even in the largest of these there are just a few hundred wolves. The species is in great danger of becoming extinct. Conservationists are striving to prevent Ethiopian wolves from dying out completely. Keeping what is left of the wolves' natural habitat is important, as is preventing domestic dogs from **breeding** with the wolves and hunting their prey. These wolves eat one species of African mole rat and mountain nyalas, like this one, also found only in the Ethiopian highlands.

Jackals

Ears pricked, the jackal turns slowly towards the tiny noise in the grass. There is little to be seen in the darkness, but the jackal does not need to see. It leaps high into the air and pounces, forefeet first. There is a short squeak, then silence as the jackal kills the rat with a bite.

Meat and vegetables

Jackals are **omnivores**: they eat both meat and plant food. Insects, eggs, fruit, vegetables and even grass are all on a jackal's menu. Jackals are also **scavengers**, often gathering in groups to pick at the remains of an animal killed by lions or other large **predators**.

Jackals hunt at night. They most often eat small animals such as **rodents**, birds and lizards, or hunt in pairs to catch larger **prey** such as rabbits, hares and antelope or gazelle fawns. Jackals will use all kinds of tricks to get food. They have been known to run in among a herd of antelope, distracting them and allowing a cheetah to get in close for the kill. The jackal then gets to eat the cheetah's leftovers.

Jackals will hang around the kill of larger predators, hoping to get the leftovers. However, only about a tenth of what they eat is **carrion**.

16

Three types

There are three different **species** of jackal – golden, side-striped and black-backed jackals. They are all medium-sized **canids**, between 30 and 50 centimetres tall at the shoulder. They are found mainly in Africa, but the golden jackal also lives in south-east Europe, the Middle East and India.

The three different kinds of jackal live in different types of **habitat**. Golden jackals usually live in dry areas, although not usually in deserts. Black-backed jackals live in grasslands and other open areas, while side-striped jackals prefer woodlands.

Family groups

Jackals usually live in pairs or small family groups rather than in packs, although they gather in large numbers when there is a good source of food.

Male and female jackals usually pair for life. Each year they find a den in which to bring up pups. Often they use an old aardvark burrow or termite mound. About 9 weeks after **mating** the female gives birth. There are usually between 2 and 9 pups. By 3 months old the pups go on hunting trips with their parents. Some young jackals leave once they have developed their hunting skills, but others stay with the family and become helpers for next year's **litter**.

Jackals hunt in pairs to catch gazelle and antelope fawns. While the mother is fending off one jackal, the other jackal sneaks up and snatches the fawn.

Jackal pups, like these side-stripes, start eating **regurgitated** food from about 2 weeks old, but they still need some milk until about 10 weeks of age.

17

Red fox

It is 3 a.m. in Bristol, UK, and a fox is on a regular patrol through its territory. Near a skip at the back of a bakery it catches a rat. In a bin outside the takeaway it finds a half-eaten pizza. Then the fox trots off to a nearby garden to raid the bird table.

A great success

Red foxes are clever and resourceful animals that can find food almost anywhere. They are among the most widespread of all land **mammals** – they live in Europe, Asia, north Africa, North America and Australia. They can survive in all kinds of **habitats**, from Arctic **tundra** to city centres.

Red foxes have been introduced into some areas by humans. European foxes were introduced into North America in the 17th century (although there were already some red foxes in the north-east of the continent). In the 19th century red foxes were also introduced into Australia.

cat-like dogs

In many ways foxes are more 'cat-like' than wolves and other 'doggy' canids (those in the **genus** Canis). For a start, they are smaller – red foxes are between 35 and 40 centimetres tall at the shoulder. They are also lighter in build, which makes them quicker and more agile. The pupils of their eyes are vertical ovals or slits, like a cat's, which gives them better night vision. Also, a fox's whiskers are much longer than in other dogs – more like those of a cat.

A red fox's large ears are good for pinpointing sounds, its cat-like eyes have good night vision and its dagger-like canine teeth can stab deep into its prey.

18

Most red foxes have reddish fur, but a small percentage have 'silver' fur (black with longer, silvery hairs), or 'cross' fur (a black stripe along the back and another across the shoulders).

Foxy words

A male fox is sometimes called a reynard. Female foxes are **vixens** and baby foxes are called **kits**. A group of foxes is called a skulk or a leash.

Hunting for prey

Foxes are best at hunting small mammals such as mice and voles, but will also hunt larger **prey** such as rabbits. When a fox hunts small prey it moves carefully and quietly, listening out for the faintest sounds. Once it hears a prey animal, the fox moves its head and ears to pinpoint exactly where the animal is. Then it launches itself into a high leap, coming down almost vertically on its prey with its front feet.

Foxes use a high 'mouse leap' when catching small animals. As youngsters they practise this kind of leaping in play.

Earthworms, fruit and dustbin scraps

A red fox's diet is not limited to small mammals. Foxes also eat prey as small as insects and worms and, in the autumn, large amounts of fruit. They also eat **carrion**, **scavenge** scraps from bird tables and root through dustbins for food.

At times when food is plentiful, a red fox caches (hides) extra food. The fox digs shallow holes and buries some food in them. A small amount of food is put into each cache, to avoid losing the whole food store if a hiding place is discovered. Red foxes have extremely good memories for where they have buried food.

Social life

Foxes are solitary hunters, but they usually live in small groups of one male and one or more females. Each group has its own territory, where it can find enough food all year round. The foxes regularly leave **scent marks** around the territory, and any intruder is driven out by force.

The **dominant** female in a group pairs with the male fox. The pair **mate** in late winter or early spring and usually 3 to 6 kits are born between February and May.

Bringing up young

As with other **canids**, fox kits are helpless at first and stay in the den with their mother. When they start to eat meat, their father and other females help to feed them. From about 4 weeks old, kits venture out of the den. At first they stay close to the entrance, but gradually they become bolder.

Foxes eat an amazing variety of food. In cities and towns they scavenge in dustbins, or eat the remains of animals killed on roads. This fox has carried off a dead squirrel.

Fox kits in their den. Female foxes usually prepare more than one den and, if any danger threatens, they move the kits to a different den.

Leaving home

The kits romp around, fighting with each other, chasing insects and pouncing on sticks. By 6 months of age they can look after themselves. The males usually leave the family group at this point, and may travel long distances to find a territory. Females tend to stay longer, and travel less far away from their birthplace.

Foxes and rabies

Foxes often suffer from the serious disease, rabies. They can spread this to dogs and sometimes even people. For many years people have tried to control rabies by killing foxes, but with limited success.

Since the 1980s, pieces of meat containing anti-rabies **vaccine** have been used to **immunize** foxes against the disease. This approach has had great success, and large parts of Europe are now rabies-free.

Millions of foxes are killed as pests each year and many more die on the roads or on railway lines. Foxes are also killed for their fur, and for sport.

Arctic fox

The Arctic fox is following a polar bear's trail. Suddenly it becomes more alert – there is a darker patch on the snow not far ahead. The fox begins to move more cautiously – it does not want to become bear food. But the polar bear has gone, leaving behind a seal carcass with plenty of meat scraps on it.

Northern home

The flat, boggy **tundra** of the far north is the natural home of the Arctic fox. It lives in northern North America, Asia and Europe, and on islands such as Greenland and Iceland. Arctic foxes are quite small, about the size of a large cat. They are between 76 and 116 centimetres in length, about a third of which is the fox's long, bushy tail.

In winter the Arctic fox has a thick, white, furry coat – it even has fur on the bottoms of its feet. In spring the Arctic foxes shed this coat for a cooler, grey-brown summer one. A few Arctic foxes have different coloured fur: these 'blue' foxes are bluish-grey in winter and chocolate-brown in summer.

A wide range of foods

The most important **prey** animals for Arctic foxes are lemmings and other **rodents**, especially in the summer. They also eat birds and their eggs, fish, berries, **carrion** and even grass and seaweed. Arctic foxes can sniff out young seal pups under the snow. They often hide or cache their food, like red foxes.

In the winter Arctic foxes often follow polar bears and scavenge their kill.

Mating and young

Before the end of the Arctic winter, male and female Arctic foxes look for partners and **mate**. After mating, the pair prepare a den for the **kits**. The female gives birth 7 or 8 weeks after mating. Arctic foxes have bigger **litters** than any other **canids** – 5 to 10 kits on average, but sometimes up to 19. The kits are helpless at first, and stay in the den for the first 3 weeks. By the age of 7 or 8 weeks they go on hunting trips, and some may leave home. Other kits do not leave until the following spring.

Arctic fox kits near their den. Good den sites are used again and again. Some sites have been in use for 300 years.

A 'blue' Arctic fox in its winter coat. The Arctic fox's coat is a better **insulator** than that of any other **mammal**.

Lots of lemmings

Feeding a large family of kits is hard work, and the male has to do much of the hunting. At first, a family of 10 or 11 kits needs 30 lemmings or equivalent food each day. This goes up to about 100 lemmings a day just before the young foxes leave home. Altogether it takes 3500 to 4000 lemmings to raise an Arctic fox family.

23

Fennec fox

A fennec fox is hunting in the Sahara Desert. Its ears prick forwards as it picks up the tiny sounds of a snake slithering over the sand. The desert viper is small, but its bite is deadly. The fox runs around the snake, biting at its head again and again. With a final bite the fox crushes the snake's skull, and carries it off to eat underground.

Smallest fox

The fennec fox is the smallest of all the **canids**. It is smaller than a rabbit, with a head and body length of between 24 and 41 centimetres. Fennec foxes live in the deserts of North Africa and in parts of the Middle East. They are **adapted** in many ways to survive the harsh desert environment.

Adapted for heat

Most canids pant to lose heat when they are hot. Saliva (spit) on the tongue **evaporates** and cools the animal down. However, a fennec fox cannot afford to lose precious liquid in this way. Instead, it loses heat through its huge ears. Blood passing through the ears loses heat into the air to help cool the fox down.

A fennec fox has a thick undercoat of fur, which keeps out the heat in the day and the cold at night.

Fennec foxes sometimes kill and eat venomous snakes such as vipers. A fennec is not immune to snakebite, but it can eat a dead snake because the venom is made harmless in its stomach.

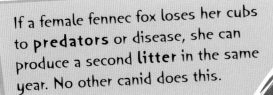
Fur on the soles of its feet stops them being burned on the hot sand. Studies suggest that fennec foxes do not need to drink at all. They get enough moisture to survive from their food.

Desert living

Fennec foxes spend the day resting in underground dens, and only become active in the cool of the evening. Because of the need to escape the desert heat, they use dens all year round, unlike most other canids.

Fennec foxes live in extended family groups of a single male and up to 9 **vixens**. The male and the **dominant** vixen **mate** early in the year, and 2 to 5 **kits** are born just over 7 weeks later. The kits are grey, rather than the sandy colour of the adults.

Night hunting

A fennec fox's ears give it superb hearing as well as helping it cool down. It can pick up the tiniest movements of **prey** in the darkness. Fennec foxes usually hunt **rodents**, such as gerbils, but they also eat a wide range of other food – rabbits, birds, snakes, lizards, insects, eggs, roots and fruit such as dates.

Bat-eared fox

On the Serengeti plains in Africa, a martial eagle swoops down towards a bat-eared fox in a tremendous dive. The fox hears the eagle coming, and begins to run. It runs fast, but not fast enough – the eagle is overtaking it. At the last moment, the fox does an almost complete about-turn, still running at full speed. The eagle misses its mark, and before it can recover the fox has escaped into its burrow.

Masked foxes

Bat-eared foxes are small, very agile, short-legged foxes with enormous ears. The head and body are 46 to 66 centimetres long, while the tail is about half this length. Bat-eared foxes live in dry grassland areas in southern and eastern Africa. They have a black 'mask' across their eyes like a racoon.

Bat-eared foxes have different teeth from other **canids**. They have at least 4 extra molars (chewing teeth), a pair in the upper jaw and a pair in the lower. These extra teeth grind up the tough outer skeletons of insects they eat.

Insect eaters

The main foods of bat-eared foxes are harvester termites and dung beetles. Both these insects are common where there are herds of grazing animals such as zebra and wildebeest. Harvester termites collect the grass that these animals eat for their underground nests.

Bat-eared foxes live close to grazing animals, because this is where they find their favourite insect foods. They also sometimes eat fruit, scorpions and small **mammals** such as mice. This fox lives in the Masai Mara Game Reserve in Kenya.

Dung beetles feed on the droppings of grazing animals and lay their eggs in balls of dung so the **larvae** have food to eat when they hatch.

Because their favourite insects are common where there are herds of large grazers, bat-eared foxes live close to these grazers too. In some areas bat-eared foxes hunt for food at night, but in southern Africa they are active during the day in winter. A bat-eared fox's hearing is so good that it can hear the sounds of beetle larvae inside balls of dung.

Family life

Bat-eared foxes live in small family groups. In areas where there is a good supply of food, these groups may live quite close to each other. Fox pairs live in burrows that they dig or take over from other animals. They may have several burrows in their **home range**, each one with several tunnels and entrances.

About 10 weeks after a pair **mate**, the **vixen** gives birth to her **kits**. There are usually between 2 and 6 kits in the **litter**. The young foxes are fully grown at 6 to 9 months old, and usually leave the family group at this age.

Bat-eared fox kits feed on their mother's milk until they are 15 weeks old. After this they begin to hunt for insects and other food.

Grey fox

Afinch is settling on its nest for the night, high in the branches of a tree. But something disturbs it: there is a **predator** nearby. Calling in alarm, the finch flies off. A few seconds later a grey fox reaches the nest and makes a meal of the finch's eggs.

Woodland foxes

Grey foxes are found from southern Canada to the northern part of South America. They are similar in size to red foxes, measuring 86 to 124 centimetres from head to tail, about a third of which is tail.

Grey foxes live mainly in woodland areas and hunt mostly at night, but they are sometimes active during the daytime. However, like other foxes they are adaptable, and are found in a wide range of **habitats**, except places that are completely treeless, including urban areas. Unlike other foxes, grey foxes are excellent tree-climbers. They have strong, hooked claws on their hind (back) feet that allow them to scramble up trees.

Varied diets

Like most other foxes, grey foxes have a varied diet. Their main **prey** animals are rabbits, mice, rats and voles. However, they also eat large numbers of insects and, in late summer and autumn, fruit is their main food. Birds and climbing animals, such as squirrels are also among the prey they creep up on.

Although grey foxes have a grizzled grey back, they have yellowish fur on their sides, reddish legs, some white on their chest and a black tip to their tail!

Island grey foxes

About 10,000 years ago, a few grey foxes found their way to the Channel Islands off the coast of California, USA. Scientists think they may have floated there on logs. Isolated from the mainland foxes, they gradually **adapted** to island life. The main difference from the mainland was that there were few larger prey animals, so the island foxes ate mostly insects.

Today, island grey foxes, like this one, are a separate **species** from those on the mainland – they are smaller and have shorter tails. Island foxes are heavily protected. Dogs, which could cause disease in the foxes, and cats, which could compete with foxes for food, are kept off the 6 islands where they live.

A den up a tree

Grey foxes use a wide range of different sites for their dens. They may use ground dens such as burrows, hollow logs or thick bushes, but sometimes dens are in hollow trees, or even old squirrel or hawk nests.

Grey foxes **mate** in early spring, and **kits** are born 7 or 8 weeks later. There are usually 3 to 5 kits to a **litter** and they are born helpless and with eyes closed. Their eyes open after 9 to 12 days, and by 3 months old they are going on hunting trips. In the late summer or autumn the family breaks up.

Zorros

On the dry **pampas** of Argentina a young lamb has lost its mother. Although it bleats pitifully, the other sheep take little notice. But another animal is very interested in the lamb. A culpeo fox, hidden by a dip in the ground, creeps slowly closer to the bleating lamb...

Wolf-like foxes

Culpeos are one of several kinds of fox found in South America. These South American foxes are known as zorros ('zorro' is the Spanish word for fox). They are stockier and more 'wolf-like' in appearance than other foxes – in fact, one 19th-century scientist called them 'fox-tailed wolves'.

Zorros are found in a wide range of different **habitats**, from deserts to rainforests. Culpeos are found in the foothills of the Andes and on the pampas of Argentina. Farmers often kill them because they hunt lambs.

Crab-eating zorros

Crab-eating zorros are found in much of northern and eastern South America. They live mainly in **savannah** grasslands, woodlands and plains. They are medium-sized foxes, about a metre long, a third of which is tail. Crab-eating zorros are grey-brown, with reddish legs and face and white underparts.

Although they are called crab-eating zorros, the land crabs that they eat are only a small part of their diet. Like most foxes they will hunt small **rodents**, but they also eat frogs and lizards, turtles' eggs, vegetables and fruit such as bananas.

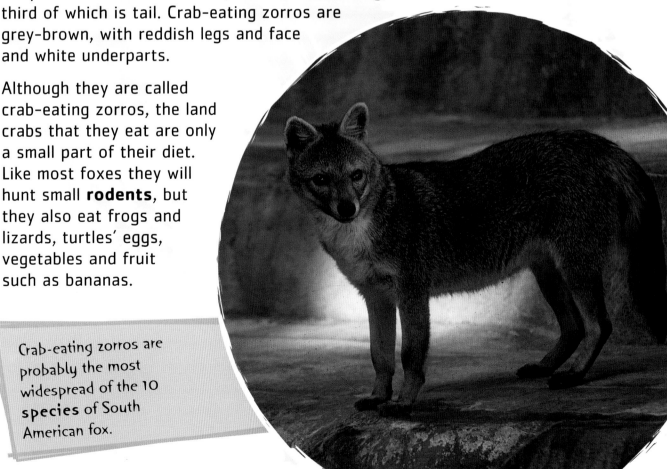

Crab-eating zorros are probably the most widespread of the 10 **species** of South American fox.

Culpeos are the largest zorros, 160 centimetres from head to tail.

Crab-eating zorros live most often in pairs. The pairs **mate** in December, and the young are born 7 to 8 weeks later. Crab-eating zorros usually use the old burrows of other animals as dens, rather than digging their own.

Three to 6 **kits** are usually born. They need their mother's milk until they are 3 months old, but by the time they reach 9 months they are adults.

Other zorros

Grey zorros, like this one, are one of the smallest zorros, sometimes only 72 centimetres from head to tail. Grey zorros have been heavily hunted for their pale grey fur. In the early 1980s, nearly half a million grey zorros were killed for the fur trade, but in recent years fewer foxes have been hunted. One zorro about which very little is known is the small-eared zorro. It is one of the few foxes that lives in rainforests.

Maned wolf

A maned wolf is out looking for food. It finds a twisted, thorny bush with large hairy leaves. The bush has fruit on it that look like yellow tomatoes. The maned wolf sniffs at the fruit and then begins to eat hungrily. This is 'fruta de lobo' (wolf's fruit), and it helps kill worm **parasites** that can grow in the wolf's gut.

A fox on stilts

The maned wolf is the biggest **canid** in South America. Although it is called a wolf, it is not a close relative of the true wolves. It looks more like a tall fox (it has been described as a 'red fox on stilts'), but it is not a true fox either – it does not have a fox's cat-like eyes, for instance.

The maned wolf is found in grasslands and river areas in eastern South America. Its coat is mainly red, but it has black 'socks' and a short black mane running down its neck and shoulders. Its long legs make it very tall: it can stand 79 centimetres at the shoulder.

Feeding

Like foxes, maned wolves are **omnivores**. About half a maned wolf's diet is wolf's fruit. The maned wolf also hunts **prey** as big as pacas – large **rodents** that can weigh 8 kilograms. However, it more often catches smaller rodents, rabbits, armadillos, birds and sometimes chickens. When catching small prey, the maned wolf pounces on them like a fox.

Maned wolves often live near rivers or in boggy areas. Their feet can splay (spread) as they walk, which stops them from sinking into wet grassland.

Night hunters

Maned wolves are usually **nocturnal**, although they also hunt in the early morning and late evening. Because of their long legs they are not good burrowers, and their dens are above ground, in thick bushes or in crevices between rocks.

Social life

Maned wolves usually live in pairs in large **territories**, which they will **scent-mark** and defend against outsiders. Within these territories the wolves are solitary, hunting and sleeping alone except during the **breeding season**.

A female maned wolf gives birth to cubs about 65 days after **mating**. The newborn cubs are blind and helpless, but they develop quickly. After 9 days their eyes and ears are open, and at 4 weeks they begin to take solid food. As among wolves and wild dogs, the adults feed the cubs at first with **regurgitated** food. By 18 weeks the young foxes no longer need their mother's milk. At a year old they are fully-grown, but they do not usually **breed** until the following year.

These maned wolf cubs are nearly fully-grown. Much of the grassland **habitat** of maned wolves has been lost and the wolves are now **endangered**.

Bush dog

A group of bush dogs is patrolling the riverbank, looking for food. One dog spots a turtle on a rock, but the turtle slips into the water. The dog plunges its head into the water, trying to find the turtle. It lifts its head out, shakes, and then plunges in again. This time it comes up with the turtle in its teeth.

Unusual canids

Bush dogs live in rainforests and wet **savannah** areas in South America. They are unusual **canids** in many ways. They have a stocky body, short legs and a stubby tail, like a terrier. But their head is more like an otter's, with a short muzzle and small, rounded ears.

The bush dog is well-**adapted** for the life it leads. Long legs would be a nuisance in the heavy undergrowth of the rainforest. Its small ears and short muzzle look like an otter's because, like the otter, it is an excellent swimmer and spends a lot of its time in water. It also has webbed feet to help it swim and dive.

Bush dogs live close to water. They are excellent swimmers and divers, and hunt some of their prey in water.

Daytime hunters

Unlike the majority of canids, bush dogs are diurnal (active during the day). They are also the most sociable of the small canids. They live in groups of up to 10 dogs, usually made up of members of the same family. At night they sleep together in a heap, hidden in a burrow or hollow tree trunk. In the morning they set off to patrol their **territory**. They run in single file, with the **dominant** female in front. The dogs 'whistle' or yelp to keep in touch. As they patrol, they **scent-mark** their regular paths. Males spray urine to scent-mark by lifting their leg, like other canids. However, female bush dogs spray a tree or other landmark by reversing up it into a 'handstand', and spraying in this position. Along their patrol route they keep a sharp lookout for possible **prey**.

Catching larger prey

Bush dogs most often hunt large **rodents** such as agoutis (fast-running relatives of guinea pigs). They also sometimes hunt in packs so they can catch prey much bigger than themselves, such as capybaras (large rodents) and ostrich-like birds called rheas. Capybaras often dive into water, but this does not help them to escape from a pack of bush dogs.

Young foxes fight among themselves for food, but bush dogs are more sociable and are happy to eat together.

Bringing up pups

Little is known about bush dog **breeding** habits. Females usually give birth to 3 or 4 pups about 2 months after **mating**. The young are dependent on their mother's milk for about 8 weeks, and by 10 months they are fully-grown.

Dingo

The fence is over 2 metres high and topped with barbed wire. It runs 5500 kilometres from the south coast of Australia to halfway up the east coast, separating the southeast corner from the rest of the continent. It is the dog or dingo fence, built to keep dingoes away from south-east Australian sheep farms.

Close to dogs

Dingoes are wild dogs, closely related to wolves and domestic (pet) dogs. They are found in Australia, South-east Asia and in New Guinea. Dingoes are not native to Australia – they were introduced into the country thousands of years ago by humans. The oldest dingo **fossil** in Australia is about 3500 years old, but dingoes are thought to have arrived much earlier than this. Dingoes are about 185 centimetres from head to tail. Most dingoes are a gingery or red colour, with white markings on the feet and chest. They live in different **habitats**, from dry deserts to rainforests. Like most **canids**, they are **nocturnal**.

Mating and young

Dingoes sometimes live in pairs, but in some areas they live in groups. Like wolves, only the **dominant** pair **mate** and produce pups. Mating takes place during the Australian autumn, and the pups are born 9 weeks later. There are typically 5 or 6 pups in a **litter**. The pups feed on their mother's milk for 2 months, and by 6 months they are independent.

Pure dingoes, like these, are usually gingery coloured, but to be certain they are pure-bred the skull and teeth have to be measured and checked.

Dingoes are adaptable hunters and will eat whatever food they can catch. This dingo is chasing a monitor lizard through the water.

Adaptable feeders

The most important **prey** animals for dingoes are kangaroos, wallabies and their relatives. Dingoes hunt wallabies alone or in pairs, but to catch larger prey, such as kangaroos, they hunt in packs. As with other canids, dingoes are adaptable feeders. In the central Australian desert, for instance, they live on lizards, rabbits and **rodents**. They also kill and eat sheep.

Threatened by dogs

Dingoes have survived many years of being hunted by humans, but more recently they have become threatened by a less obvious danger. Dingoes and domestic dogs are very closely related, and in some areas they have **bred** together. If such cross-breeding continues, the dingo will cease to exist as a separate **species**.

Killing off devils

There is strong evidence to suggest that the arrival of dingoes in Australia led to the **extinction** of two **marsupial carnivores** on the Australian mainland – the thylacine (Tasmanian tiger) and the Tasmanian devil. As their names suggest, both these animals survived on the island of Tasmania, where there were no dingoes. However, the thylacine was heavily hunted by humans in the 19th century and is now extinct.

Dhole

Crashing sounds and the whistling calls of other dholes are coming from the forest at the edge of the clearing. But the dholes waiting in the long grass stay quiet and alert. With a final crash, a large chital stag comes bounding out of the trees. Leaping from their hiding places, the dholes rush in for the kill.

Asian dogs

Dholes (pronounced 'doles') are Asian wild dogs. They are forest-dwellers, living in the steamy rainforests of India and the conifer forests of Siberia. Rainforest dholes have a thin coat of fur all year, but Siberian dholes grow a thicker coat in winter to help them survive the cold conditions.

Dholes are about the size of a collie dog, 130 to 135 centimetres long including their tail (which is about 45 centimetres long). They have a short muzzle and rounded ears.

More than most **canids**, dholes are meat-eaters. Their short muzzle gives them a powerful bite and their meat-slicing teeth (see page 4) are especially large and sharp.

Living in packs

Like wolves, dholes live in packs. An average pack has about 8 adults, with more males than females, and as many cubs. Outside the **breeding season**, several packs may gather together in 'clans' of 40 or more for a short time.

Once they have made a kill, dholes eat fast. They will defend a kill from other **predators**, even driving away tigers and bears.

Beginning a hunt

African wild dogs are crepuscular, which means that they are most active in the mornings and evenings. Like dholes, they eat large **prey**, which they hunt in packs. When the pack meets up to hunt at dawn or in the early evening, they rub and lick each other in greeting. The older dogs decide which way the pack will go, and they set off at an easy trot. The pack stays together in a loose formation, all of them on the lookout for prey.

Catching prey

When the pack finds a group of prey animals such as impala or Thompson's gazelles, they will single out a weaker individual and give chase. Over short distances gazelles can outrun wild dogs, but the dogs are tireless, and keep up the chase until their prey begin to weaken. During the hunt the dogs keep in touch with soft hooting calls.

An experienced dog can bring down a gazelle or similar-sized prey alone, but usually several dogs will be involved. The most experienced hunter will often leap at the animal's head and clamp its jaws round its lip or nose.

African wild dogs most commonly hunt medium-sized grazers, such as gazelles and antelopes, but they sometimes can hunt prey up to the size of zebra and wildebeest.

A pack of wild dogs have run this young wildebeest to a standstill. Now one of the dogs grabs the wildebeest's sensitive nose and tries to pull it down.

Social dogs

African wild dogs are highly sociable – they eat, sleep, play and hunt together. Like wolves and dholes, African wild dogs live in packs of between 2 and 30.

A pack is started when a group of sisters that have left their home pack meet up with a group of brothers (usually a larger group) that have left their home pack. One male and female establish themselves as the **dominant** pair, and the pack begins to live and hunt together.

Mating and young

Usually only the dominant pair in a pack will **mate**. The pair prepare a den (often the old burrow of a warthog or other animal) and about 10 weeks after mating the female gives birth to her pups. African bush dogs have large **litters** – the average litter size is 10. As with other **canids** the pups spend 3 weeks or so in the den. During this time the pack hunts around the den area. Once the pups are 4 or 5 weeks old, pack members help to feed them with **regurgitated** meat.

For 2 or 3 months while the pups are growing up, pack members hunt in the area of the den, so that they can bring food to the hungry youngsters.

From about 15 weeks old the pups follow the pack when they hunt. The pack now no longer returns to the den after hunting, but ranges over a much wider area. When the pack makes a kill, the youngsters are allowed to eat first. At 13 to 14 months old, African wild dogs are mature, but they stay with the pack to help with next year's pups. Females usually leave after about 2 years, but males stay on longer. Some males may stay with their home pack their whole life, but others leave after 3 years or so.

Disappearing dogs

Experts think that there are fewer than 5500 African wild dogs in the whole of Africa, and the **species** is seriously **endangered**. There are many reasons for this. But the main problem is that African wild dogs need huge amounts of space to live in, and the areas of **habitat** where they can roam freely are getting smaller and smaller. The population is split into small groups, each separated from the others. Where there are populations of 100 or more African wild dogs, the species should survive if they and their habitat are protected. But populations of 20 or fewer are unlikely to survive.

African wild dogs need a **territory** of least 400 square kilometres (150 square miles). In areas where food is scarce each pack may need a territory of 2000 square kilometres (770 square miles).

43

classification chart

Scientists classify living things by comparing different kinds and deciding how closely related to each other they are. They then sort the millions of different living things into groups. Different **species** of living things that are closely related are put together in a larger group called a **genus** (plural genera). Similar genera are grouped into **families**, and similar families are grouped together in orders. Closely related orders are grouped into classes, classes are grouped into phyla and phyla are put together in huge groups called kingdoms. Wolves and dogs make up the **canid** family (Canidae) within the order Carnivora (**carnivores**). Carnivores belong to the class Mammalia (**mammals**).

Canid genera

Genus	Number of species	Examples
Wolves and 'true' dogs (Canis)	9	wolf, domestic dog, dingo, jackals, coyote, Ethiopian wolf
Grey foxes (Urocyon)	2	grey fox, island grey fox
Bat-eared foxes (Otocyon)	1	bat-eared fox
Foxes (Vulpes)	12	red fox, fennec fox, Arctic fox
Zorros (Dusicyon)	8	culpeo zorro, crab-eating zorro
African wild dogs (Lycaon)	1	African wild dog
Dholes (Cuon)	1	dhole
Maned wolves (Chrysocyon)	1	maned wolf
Bush dogs (Speothos)	1	bush dog
Racoon dog (Nyctereutes)	1	racoon dog
Small-eared dogs (Atelocynus)	1	small-eared dog

Where wolves and dogs live

These maps show where some of the wolves and dogs in this book live.

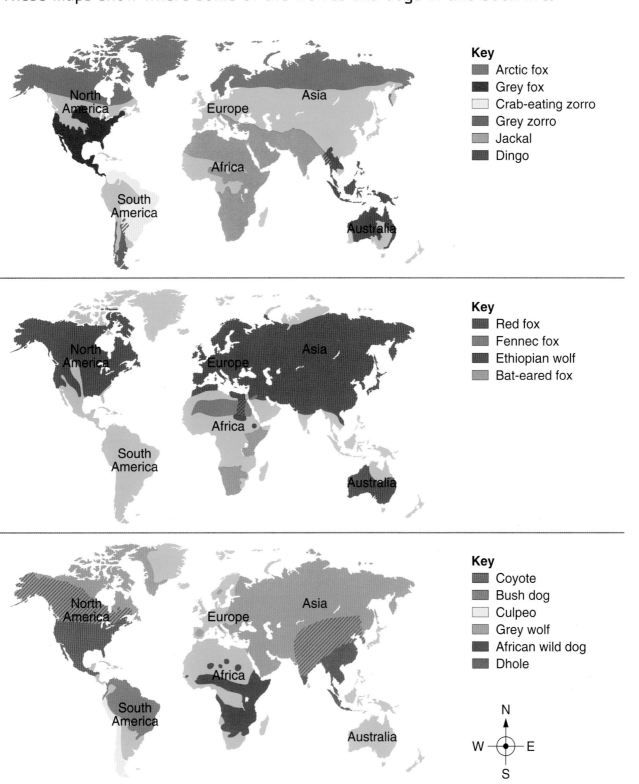

Key
- Arctic fox
- Grey fox
- Crab-eating zorro
- Grey zorro
- Jackal
- Dingo

Key
- Red fox
- Fennec fox
- Ethiopian wolf
- Bat-eared fox

Key
- Coyote
- Bush dog
- Culpeo
- Grey wolf
- African wild dog
- Dhole

Glossary

adapted special features organisms have to help them live in their habitat

breed when animals breed they mate and produce young

breeding season some animals breed only at a certain time each year: their breeding season

canids family of mammals that includes dogs, wolves and foxes

carnivore meat-eater

carrion dead and rotting meat

descendants the offspring of an animal: their children, grandchildren and so on

domesticated trained to live with people

dominant more powerful or important

endangered when an animal is in danger of becoming extinct (dying out)

evaporate when water turns from a liquid to a gas, it evaporates

extinct/extinction when a whole species of living things die out

family group or genera of living things that are closely related

fossil remains of an animal or plant that have been in the ground for many years and have become hard like rock

genus (plural genera) group of species of living things that are closely related

habitat place where an animal lives

hibernate to go into a deep sleep through the winter

home range area in which an animal or group of animals lives

hybrid animal or plant produced by breeding together two different species

immunize give a medicine or injection to protect against disease

inbreeding when closely related animals breed together. Inbreeding can cause young to be weak or deformed.

insulator material that stops heat passing through it

kit young fox

larva (plural larvae) the young stage of an insect

litter young born to a female in one birth

livestock farm animals, such as cattle

mammal hairy, warm-blooded animal that feeds its young on breast milk

marsupial mammal such as a kangaroo, which has a pouch where its babies grow and develop after birth

mate (noun) partner of the opposite sex that an animal breeds with

mating (verb) when a male and a female animal come together to produce young

nocturnal active at night

omnivore animal that eats both meat and plant food

pampas wide grasslands in South America

parasite creature that lives and feeds on or in another living creature, without giving any benefit in return

predator animal that hunts and eats other animals

prey animals that are hunted by predators

regurgitate bring up food that has already been swallowed

rodent mammal with large, chisel-like front teeth, such as a rat or a squirrel

savannah grassland with scattered bushes and trees

scavenger animal that sometimes eats carrion and waste material

scent-marking marking a territory with urine or droppings

species group of animals that are similar and can breed

territory area around an animal's home that it defends from other animals of the same species

tundra cold, bleak lands that are covered with snow for most of the year

vaccine a medicine that stimulates the body's defences against a particular disease

vixen female fox

Further Information

Books

Foxes, Wolves and Wild Dogs of the World, David Alderton (Blandford, 1994)
A good reference book covering all kinds of wolves and wild dogs.

Wild Dogs: Wolves, Coyotes and Foxes, Deborah Hodge (Kids Can Press, 1997)
An easy-to-read information book for young students.

Running with the Fox, David Macdonald (HarperCollins, 1987)
An excellent, entertaining book on foxes by one of the world's experts.

Life in a Pack of Wolves, Louise and Richard Spilsbury (Heinemann Library, 2003)
A basic overview of wolves and the pack.

Once a Wolf: How Wildlife Biologists Fought to Bring Back the Gray Wolf
Stephen R Swinburne (Houghton Mifflin, 1999)
The story of the troubled relationship of wolves with humans.

The Wild Side of Pet Dogs, Jo Waters (Raintree, 2004)
Presents the lives of pet dogs, showing the close links to their wild ancestors.

Websites

www.canids.org
The Canids Specialist Group website on canids. Contains articles and conservation information on most species.

http://mynarskiforest.purrsia.com/ev1con.htm
Liska's Encyc*Vulpedia*. An enjoyable and interesting site all about foxes.

www.rudimentsofwisdom.com/themes/themes_animals.htm
The Rudiments of Wisdom. This wonderful cartoon encyclopedia has articles on dogs, foxes and wolves.

www.pbs.org/wgbh/nova/wolves/
NOVA Online: Wild Wolves. Listen to some wolf howls, learn about how wolves have been reintroduced into parts of North America, and learn about the dog–wolf connection.

Index

Titles in the *Wild Predators!* series include:

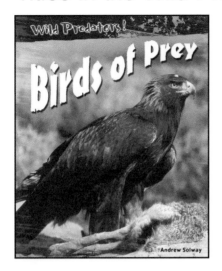

Hardback   0 431 18992 7

Hardback   0 431 18994 3

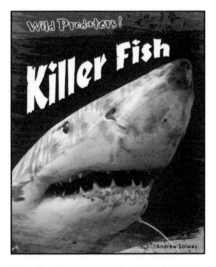

Hardback   0 431 18991 9

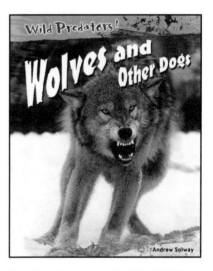

Hardback   0 431 18995 1

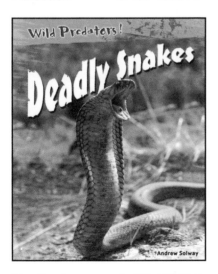

Hardback   0 431 18993 5

Find out about the other Heinemann Library titles on our website www.heinemann.co.uk/library